Rules for the other side.

By

Trouble

Dedication

Acknowledgment

About The Author

Table of Contents

Being a side chick comes in many different forms. You don't have to be sleeping with another woman's man to be a side chick—there are many ways to be one beyond that. But if that is the case for you, then so be it. Who am I to judge? No one, that's who. And fuck anyone who makes you feel wrong or tries to judge you for the choices you make in your life. It's your life and your path, and you are the one who has to walk it. If this is the path you choose, then so be it.

But here is a list of rules you need to follow to be a good one and to have an easier time walking the path you've chosen. Just do me one favor. Keep in mind that just like you picked this path, you can always choose a different one later on if you want to. That decision is entirely up to you.

Before you go down this path, take the time to ask yourself these questions. Remember, for this to work, you have to be open and honest with yourself when answering. If you can't do that, please close this book and find something safe to do because this path is not for you. You could end up hurting yourself or someone else, and I would hate for that to happen.

Baby, this world is not what it used to be—people are crazier than ever. I would hate for you to become a TikTok page or a face on an R.I.P. shirt. No one has the time or money for that. So, if you're not ready, put this book down.

Now, onto the questions.

1. Do you know who you are as a person?

2. Are you an emotional person?

3. Are you mentally stable?

4. How do you handle being alone?

5. How good are you at controlling your emotions?

6. What's your attitude style?

7. How good are you at sharing?

8. How is your self-esteem?

9. Are you easy to get attached to a person?

These are just a few of the questions you need to ask yourself if this is the path you want to take because how you answer them will determine if being a side chick is right for you. Not everyone is meant to be a side chick, and that's okay. Everything isn't for everybody, which is why *you need to know* yourself and who you truly are.

Rule Number 1
Don't Fall for the Dick

Rule number one of being a side chick is to never, ever—never *ever*—and I do mean *ever* in your life, fall for the dick. You do just enough to be better than the main chick but not so much that you start catching feelings for him.

Now, when I say *catch feelings*, I don't mean you can't care about him. You do care—you care about the money and the dick you get from him. Anything more than that, and you're not the side chick—you're the mistress. And if that's the case, you need to be getting everything the main chick is getting *and more.*

Falling for the dick is a *bad* idea. By doing this, you're opening a door that allows you to get hurt—not just emotionally but physically as well. Because you never know what he's telling *her*, just like she doesn't know what he's telling *you.* And at the end of the day, you will *always* be the bad guy. Even when it's the man's fault, you will still be blamed—in her eyes and everyone else's.

We live in a world where a man can be wrong but still be right at the same time. I know that sounds crazy coming from someone writing a book about *rules for side chicks,* but this is the world you live in. And as women, we *should* do a better job of sticking together and uplifting each other—but that's not the world we live in. That's not how things work. It's a dog-eat-dog world out here, and if you let it, it will break you—or even kill you.

So to prevent that, *please don't fall for the dick.* I don't want to see anyone go through the pain of heartbreak over a man who wasn't good enough for them anyway. And *that* is exactly what will happen if you catch feelings for someone else's man—because that's what he is: *someone else's man.*

I don't care how much he tells you he loves you or how *different* you are. He is not going to leave his girl for you.

Now, disclaimer: I *have* seen cases where a man actually left his girl to be with his side chick. But in those cases, the side chick was *once* the main chick, and he was never really over her; she still had a place in his heart.

But that may *not* be the case for you. And if it's not, don't get your hopes up. Keep your guard up.

Also, the *I love you* does *not* count if he says it while you're having sex. I hate to break it to you, sweetheart, but he's enjoying the sex— it's not really *you* he's talking about in that moment.

Getting yourself emotionally involved will lead you to do things that are out of your lane, which can create more problems for you later. It will also make it harder for you to let go and move on when it's time— because you'll become *attached* to that man.

And that's something you *cannot* do.

At any given moment, he can walk away, leaving you feeling played and hurt—all because you fell in love with him and started planning a life for the two of you, forgetting that you were never his main girl…

or even his girl *at all.*

Then you'll start wanting to do things that are outside of a side chick's lane, like cooking for him and taking care of him.

That is *not* your job. That is *out* of your zone.

That's the main chick's job—so let *her* do just that. Let *her* take care of the little things. Your role? Get the dick, go out, and have fun. That's it.

Below is a list of things you should *never* do as a side chick:

- Cuddling

- Holding hands

- Cooking (*This one isn't really on the list, but it's on the list— meaning, no cooking his meals every time you see him unless he's the one putting food in the house every two weeks.*)

- Cleaning

- Washing his clothes

- Helping him financially (*Unless you both agree that he's paying you back with interest.*)

- Buying him gifts (*It's his job to buy you gifts—unless it's Christmas or maybe his birthday.*)

- Helping take care of his kids

- Helping with his family's issues

- Dealing with his mother, father, siblings, cousins, or friends

This is *not* your man. DO NOT TREAT HIM LIKE YOUR MAN.

I repeat—THIS IS NOT YOUR MAN.

Do not get in the habit of acting like he is because if you do, he will *use that against you*, and you'll only end up hurting yourself in the long run.

And as the side chick, you are not in the game to get hurt.

Let his girl do all that shit. *You* are here to have fun—so do just that. Have fun.

Rule Number 2
Don't Get Played for a Fool

This rule is really simple. If you're the type of person who just wants the dick for yourself, that's fine—there's nothing wrong with that. *Really, it's not.*

But I'm going to be completely honest with you. And if you're the type of person who *can't* handle honesty, then maybe you should close this book and put it back—because this book is not for you.

And FYI, you are dumb. Dumb as hell.

I'm sorry—I know that was a mean thing to say, but *damn*, someone needs to be the one to tell you. And clearly, your friends aren't as honest as I am. Hell, *maybe* they are, but you're too damn hardheaded to see it.

And I hate to be the one to break it to you, but you are dumb as fuck and need to see a doctor to have your brain checked—because you have the game *fucked up* in a major way.

Now, don't get me wrong—I'm not telling you to be a gold digger or only get with a guy for his money or what he can do for you. But at the end of the day, this is a business transaction. He wants to fuck. You have bills. Or, depending on what type of man he is, he might even help you get a better job. Who knows? This could go a lot of ways—which we'll talk about later.

So, let's look at it this way:

If a guy comes over to *your* house—a house where *you* pay all the bills and he stays for the weekend, he's going to eat, drink, shit, and shower there, right?

Which means:

- He's using *your* lights.

- He's drinking *your* juice and soda.

- He's eating *your* food and snacks.

- He's running up *your* bills.

Yes, *you* asked him over for the weekend—but that means there's now *less* food and drinks in *your* place. And if you have kids, that's *less* snacks for *them.*

All for something you could literally buy online or at the store, *and it would be all yours.*

I can't speak for you, but *me*? I want my money back.

Don't *you* want your money back?

Hell, dick isn't paying these bills. And the cost of living is only getting higher. You know it, and I know it—the government is no real help.

If you *still* can't see it that way because you're like, *but I asked him over*, then think about it this way:

You wake up to go to work. Some people get paid every two weeks, right?

That means you have to get up at 6 or 7 AM to be at work by 8 AM. Then you're there, working for 8 to 9 hours, depending on your job.

Now, let's say you have to work an extra 4 hours of overtime. You look forward to that money on your check, right?

But when payday comes, you check your pay stub and see that those 4 hours of overtime are missing.

Do you have the right to act a fool and demand your money? Or would you just let it slide and take the loss?

Hell no!

You want *your* money, right?

Because *I* sure as hell want mine. All of it.

I don't work for free. What the *hell* is wrong with you?

Shit, I have kids (only two—and they are so cute), and they cost money. Times are *hard* and only getting harder. So I'll be *damned* if I let someone come into my home and take from them—especially when that person has a whole-ass job and isn't even my man.

Hell no. Fuck no. Run me my money.

Fuck, you mean?

Rule Number 3
You Will Never Replace the Main

Don't think for a second that you're going to replace the main chick.

Your job as the side chick is to be everything that the main girl is not. A good side chick knows her place and how to stay in it.

When holidays come up, please don't expect him to be around or to call you—because *that* is family time, and he will be with his family. And as the side chick, you are not family.

Point blank, period.

Sorry, someone had to tell you. Sorry, it had to be me. But there it is.

- As the side chick, you do not get the same benefits as the main chick. That means:

- If the dick passes away, please do not—and I *mean* DO NOT—show up at the funeral acting a fool.

- Do not try to be seen.

- Do not tell anyone who will listen that you were fucking that man three nights a week.

- And for the love of God, do not go around telling people he liked a finger up his ass to come.

That's too much information for *anyone* but *you and him.*

Shitty fingers.

1. You will only make yourself look like an ass.

2. Get ready to get jumped by his daughters, his mama, his sister, his auntie—and hell, even some of his cousins might jump in just for fun.

So that's a NO-NO.

Next, do not expect to be in the man's will.

Collect yours before he passes, or be smart about it:

- Get some shit in writing.

- Have it notarized.

- Make it a legal document.

If you're *really* thinking ahead, you could even take out a life insurance policy on him. That's the *gift that keeps on giving* if you ask me. *No shade.*

But for real—some of you side chicks need to think outside the box.

And if you're going for something big, please:

1. Make sure it's in your name.

2. Make sure you can afford it if he hasn't paid it off yet.

3. At the very least, make sure half of it is paid off so you don't have much left to cover.

4. Be physically present when he puts it in your name.

Never fall for the, *"Oh baby, I got you—it's in your name, you good."*

Hell no.

I need papers in my hand, sweetie. Or it's a no-go.

Because these men lie.

And the next thing you know, wifey has your shit towed for fun, or she's fucking up your shit every other day. And best believe replacing shit ain't cheap.

Windows, whether on a car or a house are expensive.

And if wifey is busting those bitches out, then he needs to be:

- Paying you more

- Moving you to a new place

- Replacing your shit

- Compensating you for the harassment you're receiving because of him

Because we do not want any of that.

And if you have any friends like me, then the answer is hell no, we do not.

I look good in orange, but it's not a color I'm trying to wear *every day.*

You feel me?

So act like you got some sense—the *good Lord* gave you some.

Know your place.

Rule Number 4
Taking Care of Your Glitter Box

Rule #4 is VERY important as a side chick—but honestly, as a female in general.

It is very important that you take care of your glitter box.

(I got the name from my friend at work—don't ask me why she calls it that, but she does. And having a daughter myself, I thought it was a good name to use.)

Your glitter box should be cleaned daily, with a deep clean once a week.

Now, I should not have to tell people this, but I've heard enough stories to know that I do.

So, I'm about to go step by step on:

- How to clean your glitter box.

- How to take care of your glitter box.

How to Clean Your Glitter Box

Your glitter box is your pussy, and it should be cleaned regularly:

- Once a day in the winter.

- Twice a day in the summer (because y'all know it gets hot and sweaty).

Wash with soap and water.

(Now, everyone's body is different, and some people can't use certain soaps or body washes. If that's you, then don't use them. Listen to your body.)

I personally use Dial soap—I like the cranberry Dial to clean with.

Once a week, I also:

- Take a hot bath with vinegar.

- Take an oil bath to keep my skin moisturized.

Because no one likes a female with dry-ass, rough-ass skin.

So please—after you bathe, rub your body down with some type of lotion or oil.

How to Take Care of Your Glitter Box

Your mother should have taught you this as a kid, but let's go over it again:

- Wipe from front to back—not back to front. (*Don't play with infections.*)

- Wash her well—part those lips and clean all your folds.

- Just like you like to smell and taste a clean dick, men want to eat some clean pussy—so wash her well.

Now, let's talk hair.

I'm not saying you have to cut all your hair off (unless that's what you like), but at least keep it neat.

- Take some Nair and shape it up.

- It's better for you, too—because after he's done eating you out, he might kiss your ass (*literally*), and if you've got a bush, you might end up with hair in your mouth.

And just like you don't want that shit in your mouth—what makes you think he wants that shit in his?

So, make sure your shit is done before he gets there or before you get to his place.

Also—very important:

- Do NOT use Nair five minutes before he's about to go down there.

- That shit smells.

- And it also leaves a little bit behind.

Taking Care of Your Glitter Box

Now, to take good care of your glitter box, keep this in mind: You are what you eat.

No, I'm not talking about your weight—I mean the food you eat and what you drink. Everything you put in your mouth has to come out somewhere, and your glitter box is that somewhere.

So, watch what you eat.

Now, I'm not saying you can't eat fast food, but you should watch how much of it you eat at a time.

No one likes to eat a whole lot of salt, and if you eat too much fatty food, that's what you're going to taste like.

To keep your glitter box tasty and clean it out from all that fatty, greasy food, make sure to eat healthy every now and then.

True Story: Why It's Good to Keep a Clean and Healthy Glitter Box

Me and my friends went to a house party.

Now, I didn't know this chick—never met her a day in my life before this.

But you could smell her before you saw her.

At the time, they were cooking fish, so I guess people just thought it was the fish—but I'm too damn good at my job to not pick up on this.

That chick smelled like she hadn't bathed or showered in weeks.

All you could smell was fish.

And then this chick sat down beside me.

Now, for all of you who don't know, I am that friend—the one you have to watch in public because you never know what I will say or do.

But this chick caught me on a good day.

I just looked at her and asked, "Are you getting in the pool?"

When she said, "Yeah," I asked, "When?"

Because the minute her ass hit the water, I was gonna throw some soap on that ass.

Because there is no way—as a female, as a damn person—you should leave the house smelling like that.

Period.

But let's continue.

As the party went on, more and more people started to question where the fish smell was coming from.

The whole time?

It was her.

And she was just walking around like she didn't smell shit.

Then, she started talking to this guy I know, and he went to sit between her legs.

He jumped back and asked, "Did you eat any fish today? Or were you helping to cook the fish?"

She said, "No, why?"

He pushed her ass in the pool and said, "Your ass stinks. Wash your ass."

Long story short: Don't be her.

Clean your ass.

No one wants a sour pocket—it's just not cute.

Before I Forget...

If you are going to do any of these things, make sure to:

1 CHECK WITH YOUR DOCTOR.

Because by no means am I a doctor, and I do not know any of you personally.

I don't know what you're allergic to or how sensitive your skin is, so PLEASE:

DON'T USE ANYTHING YOU'RE NOT SUPPOSED TO.

TALK TO YOUR DOCTOR ABOUT IT FIRST.

Step-by-Step Guide: What I Use and How I Use It

Now, this is just me—I'm not telling you to do this because everybody's body is different, and you have to know what works for you.

But here's what I do and a list of the things I use.

You should have most of these items in your house, but if not, it's okay.

What You Need:

- Dial soap (*gold bar*)
- Goat milk or whole milk
- All-natural raw honey
- Apple cider vinegar
- Epsom salt
- Listerine (*the blue one*)
- Vaseline or deep moisturizer

- Sugar scrub (*of your choice*)

- A face cleanser

- Four cans of pineapple juice

- Two of whatever type of fruit or candy you like

Now that you have the items from the list, this is how I use them to make my skin feel baby-soft and how I make myself taste so good.

Let's start by cleaning the fruit and placing two cans of pineapple juice in the freezer.

While the juice is chilling and the fruit is drying after being cleaned, you will start by taking a hot shower.

You don't need it to be burning hot, but it should be hot enough to ensure you're getting clean.

Next, take Dial soap and wash your body.

I do not use a regular wash rag—I have an African exfoliating rag (*PS: My best friend got me this one year for Christmas, and I never looked back!*).

After you have completely washed your body twice, you can move on to the next step: exfoliating your skin.

Take your sugar scrub and wash your body down with it—this will help prepare your skin for a milk bath.

Now, this type of bath is something I do once a month to keep my skin soft and moisturized, and it's really easy to do.

Just take one cup of milk and a tablespoon of honey, then heat it for 60 seconds or until it's warm.

While waiting for the milk to heat up, make sure to wash down the tub to get it ready for the bath.

When preparing the bathwater, sprinkle in a little Epsom salt and stir it up.

Soak in the tub for a few minutes, then get out and clean the tub to prepare for the milk bath.

For both baths, make sure the water is hot enough. If you can handle it a little hotter, go for it!

If you can take the water a little hotter, go for it!

Now, for the milk and honey, you'll need a measuring cup. Pour in one cup of milk and two teaspoons of honey, then heat it up in the microwave.

Do not boil the milk, just warm it enough to melt the honey.

Before pouring it into the bathwater, make sure to stir it well.

Now, soak in the bath until the water gets cold.

Make sure to bring a book or turn on some music. I personally love listening to soft jazz or '90s R&B to help me relax.

Of course, this is completely up to you—this is just what I love to do to keep my skin soft and moisturized.

When you're done with both baths (or just the milk bath), it's time to dry off and apply your favorite lotion or moisturizer. I personally love Vaseline.

Once that's done, it's time to start drinking your pineapple juice and water.

Foot Care Routine

Now, I'm sure you go to the salon to get your feet and nails done, but if not, here's a little trick to keep your feet soft between visits.

You can use your tub or a foot spa—just heat the water to your preferred temperature. But before adding the water, pour in the following:

- 1 cup of Listerine

- ½ cup of apple cider vinegar

- Epsom salt (I don't measure this exactly, but if I had to guess, about ¾ of a cup should do)

Mix these together, then add your warm/hot water and soak your feet for about 20 minutes. After soaking, wash your feet off, apply moisturizer, and put on socks until you're ready for bed.

Face Care Routine

By this time, you should be ready to do your face routine. Grab your facial cleanser, tie your hair back (or wrap it up), and start your skincare routine.

If you don't have a routine, you need to start one—trust me, it helps your skin in the long run!

Final Steps

Once everything is done, relax with your pineapple juice and snack on some fruit while you pack your fruit, juice, and water for the morning.

Now, here's the deal:

- You'll be eating fruit and drinking a lot of water for the next two weeks.

- But when it comes to pineapple juice, drink four cans, then take a break.

- Pineapple has a lot of acid, and drinking too much can make your lips and tongue go numb!

Rule Number 5
The Benefits and Disadvantages of Being a Side Chick

When it comes to this rule, I need you to understand that yes, there are both advantages and disadvantages to being a side chick. The impact depends on the type of person you are and where you are in life—that will determine how you view your options.

For some, being a side chick comes with a lot of disadvantages, such as:

- You're alone a lot.

- During holidays, you have no one to share them with outside of your family or friends.

- Those cute couple photos? You can take them, but you better not post them.

- If you're ever in trouble, you don't have a man to call for help in the middle of the night.

- Unless you have kids, you go home to an empty house.

- On cold winter nights, your bed is really cold, and you have to clear off your car after the snow by yourself.

- You don't get the same advantages as the main chick.

But there are some plus sides to being a side chick, including:

- You don't have to answer to anyone but yourself.

- You don't have to worry about anyone else's feelings but your own.

- You are free to work on yourself and heal.

- You avoid a lot of the drama that comes with some guys.

- You get to do something that many people don't get to do— you get to truly know WHO you are as a person.

At the end of the day, you just have to worry about and focus on yourself. And I'm not just talking about taking care of yourself physically—I mean mentally and emotionally as well. You have to take time for yourself to make sure you're okay because if you don't, you can lose yourself—and that's the last thing you want to do.

Being a side chick is not easy, and at times, it can even lead to feeling depressed. Now, I know some of you are thinking, "No one asked you to be a side chick," or "No one made you do it." And honestly? You're right.

But people become side chicks for different reasons. We may not agree with them or like them, but we have to respect them. We don't know why someone made that choice.

There are a number of reasons why someone might become a side chick:

- They're taking a break from long-term relationships and just want a friends-with-benefits situation until they're ready to commit again.

- They may be over relationships altogether and just want to have fun.

At the end of the day, no one truly knows what's going on in a person's head but them. Their reasons are their own, and that's their choice to make.

Rule Number 6
Have some class, don't look like an ass—know your place and how to play the game.

Just because you're a side chick doesn't mean you can't be classy. No one wants a side chick who can't play her part and take the high road.

Ladies, if you're ever out and the main catches you, your job is to sit there and look cute. Don't be running off at the mouth or putting your business out there, just let her do all the talking.

Now, watch her body language—because if she looks like she's about to hit you and you feel like she's about to hit you—then damn it, bitch, duck or move! She is going to hit you, so you need to be ready at all times.

By doing all that yelling and moving around, she's going to be short of breath and low on energy because she's too busy attacking him by yelling and crying. That gives you the advantage if it ever comes down to a fight.

Now, if you must fight the main chick, then he needs to be paying you more—and you need to understand that he's going to leave with her. So, make sure that if you guys go out, you drive your own car. If not, he better have Cash App'd you at least $200 so you have a way to get home.

After you get home, don't be mad if you don't hear from him for a few days. Wifey is going to be on his ass like white on rice, so take this time to relax and do you.

Use this time to chill, hang out with your friends, and get your hair and nails done. Yes, you have to keep yourself up at all times.

So, go soak in a hot bath with water and vinegar to clean out your glitter box and relax your muscles from all that stress and drama.

FLY.

Now, this may not be for everyone, but you might want to try a Yoni Steam to help tighten your glitter box back up and clean it out, too.

Being a side chick is like running your own business.

You always have to play it smart and do what's in your best interest— which means you look out for yourself at all times. No one is going to look out for you better than you.

With that being said, never team up with the wife unless it benefits you. Go where the money is. If the husband has the money, then you're on his side. If the wife has the money, then you're on her side. You are about your money at all times—period, point blank.

If at any time you don't understand this, please go back and reread rule number one. Better yet, let me help you even more—don't work for free. Hell, wrong with you?

If you didn't know, being a side chick is a full-time job. Some people may not feel that way, but yes, it is. You may not pay taxes for being a side chick, but you do have to work at it—and sometimes, you have to put in long hours. Some side chicks put in 10-hour days, and that doesn't even count overtime.

As a side chick, you work 365 days a year. It's a never-ending job.

Now, you may be thinking, "Once he goes home to wifey, my job is done."

The answer to that is Hell No.

Some side chicks have more than one at a time. Now, if you're a beginner, we understand—start with one to see if this is your thing. If it's not, that's okay.

Not everyone can be a side chick because it's a hard job.

Rule Number 7
The Types of Side Chicks

There are many types of side chicks out there, and they come in different forms. In this section, we're going to break down the different types and define each one—so you can see which type of side chick you want to be or which type you may already have.

The main types are:

- The Classy (Business) Side Chick

- The Trashy Side Chick

- The Crazy Side Chick

- The Undercover (Quiet) Side Chick

- The Baby Mama Side Chick

- The Friend Side Chick

The Classy Side Chick

A Classy Side Chick is a lady who knows her place and how to play the game. She will not call your phone—she waits for you to reach out. If you see her out in public, you don't have to worry about her acting a fool or putting your business out there for the world to see.

She's all about her business—and if you get your shit together, she's with it. If not, she will cut your ass off quickly. She may even hit you with a contract—which we'll get into later in the book.

The Trashy Side Chick

A Trashy Side Chick can go one of two ways:

1. She can level up and become a lower-tier Classy Side Chick—cool and laid-back until you push her to that point.

2. She can flip out and turn into a Crazy Side Chick, which means things will get wild for everyone involved.

The Crazy (Gold Digger) Side Chick

A Crazy Side Chick is one that requires a lot of money—because she's unpredictable.

Think of her like a present: the box looks good, it's the right size, and it has all the right colors to make you want it. But once you unwrap it, it may not be what you expected—and sometimes, it's more than you can handle.

The Undercover (Quiet) Side Chick

Now this chick is a pro.

She has all the skills of the Classy Side Chick, the Trashy Side Chick, and the Crazy Side Chick—but you would never know she was the side chick because she knows how to hide in plain sight.

She doesn't run her mouth, so she could be his best friend, his co-worker, or even your sister—and because she's so low-key, you wouldn't even suspect her.

The Friend Side Chick

This type of side chick is a catch-22.

She could be a real friend that he just happened to sleep with (or still is from time to time). But he keeps her around because she's a good friend to him.

Now, if that's the case, it's going to be hard to tell if he's still messing with her or not.

Your Best Friend's Side Chick

Now, this chick is a hot mess—and she is not really your friend.

If you ever find yourself in a situation like this, the best move is to cut both of them out of your life. She's wrong for not following girl code, and he's wrong for being that damn messy.

The Baby Mama Side Chick

This type of side chick is difficult to deal with—because while she's the mother of his kids, the father and her are not together.

But the problem is, he keeps going back when he's single or separated, which gives her false hope that they will eventually get back together.

The Work Wife/Girlfriend Side Chick

This is the chick at his/her job who plays the role of the main and acts like the main when the actual main isn't around.

She thinks she's more important than she actually is and expects to be treated like the main. Hell, some of them even act that way in front of the main chick—but they like to play it off as a joke.

The Friend of the Family / Blast from the Past Side Chick

Now, this one is tricky.

She's a friend of the family and knows everyone—so the family treats her like a sister. Because of that, she always has an open invitation to family events, making it easier for her to stick around without raising suspicion.

Rule Number 8
The Contract

The contract is a document between the side chick and the dick—and this document is very important.

It determines how long the side chick and the dick will interact with each other. Typically, the contract lasts between 6 to 12 months—because anything longer than that, you might as well be the main chick.

Inside this contract, you'll outline:

- What you are willing to do and what you are not willing to do

- Whether he's the only one you're fucking or if you're free to see other niggas

I'm sure you've seen *Fifty Shades of Grey*—and if not, go watch the movie. It might be PG to me, but it does touch on some things you need to know about what to include in a contract like this.

But remember, a contract isn't just about money or gifts. It's there to protect you, make sure you're safe, and ensure that both parties are covered.

This is legal documentation that both parties must review and agree on. If both parties do not sign the document and cannot come to an agreement, then walk away from the dick—because if something happens to you, it's all on you.

Make sure you also get the document notarized and keep your copy somewhere safe. That way, if things get out of hand, you have something to protect yourself with.

By getting it notarized, this is what makes it a legal document. Make sure to keep the document somewhere safe where you can access it at any time.

When reviewing the contract, PLEASE do not hesitate to speak up about anything you like or don't like before signing. Once you sign, there is no going back on anything in it. If you're unsure about anything, ask as many questions as you need to fully understand what's expected of you.

If necessary, take the contract and review it for a few days to make sure you completely understand it. Do your research on anything that seems unclear.

This contract should include:

1. Term

How long the agreement will last. Most side chicks do one year before moving on.

Clearly state the Start Date and End Date.

2. Compensation

- I'll say this again for the slow people in the back—MAKE SURE YOU GET YOUR MONEY.

- No IOUs. Payment must be Cash, CashApp, or Zelle ONLY.

- Include exact payment dates and how payments will be made.

If part of the deal includes him buying you a house or car, make sure it's in YOUR NAME and YOUR NAME ALONE.

Rule Number 9
When It Comes to the Main Chick

When you're with the dick and **the** main chick calls, don't get mad at him for saying he's out with his friends or working late at the office. You **knew** he had a wife/girlfriend at home when you first started talking to him, so don't act brand new now.

And don't get mad if he goes into another room or tells you to be quiet when she calls. You better not get upset if he tells her he loves her on the phone in front of you, either—because at the end of the day, you're just some ass on the side. That doesn't mean he doesn't care about you, but he's not in love with you.

And if you didn't know, there are different types of love out here. When someone cares about you, it might be more on a friend level, not a deep, romantic kind of love. So there's no need to get in your feelings if he says he's out with his friends—because technically, you are out, and you are a friend. He's not really lying, but at the same time, he's not telling the whole truth either—and that's not your place to get into.

The main chick will always come first, even if he says he's not happy or it's not like that at home. Home always comes first—because if it didn't, his ass would've been left. But he hasn't, which means she must be doing something right to keep him around.

Main Chicks, This Is for You

Just because you're the main chick doesn't mean you can't be replaced by the side chick. It has happened before—where the main chick became the side chick, and the side chick became the main. So get down off that high horse and stop thinking you can't be replaced—because you can. And if **you** don't get your shit together, you could be replaced by the side chick.

Being a side chick can sometimes be a very hard job because he's not always going to be there for you. You have to understand that home comes first. And as much as he may want to be with you, he can't just leave to be with you.

Now, as the side chick, you must understand that he can and will only call or text you when **he's** not around the main chick, his kids, or their family—which includes any close friends you may have met.

And in case you didn't know, as a side chick, you should never mix business with pleasure. His family should not know you, and you should not know them—that's how trouble starts. Getting too close to his family or friends is a huge mistake. Trust and believe—if anyone in his family can identify you in any way, best believe they'll use that to their advantage, and shit will start going downhill fast.

So cut that shit off before it even starts. You don't need to know anyone—and they don't need to know you.

Rule Number 10
How to Deal with Your Emotions / Keep Your Mouth Shut

If you know you are an emotional person, then being a side chick is not for you. You'll have a hard time controlling your emotions, which can make things messy and cause things to end badly. You have to be able to cut your emotions off and stop yourself from falling for the dick—if you can't do that, this life isn't for you.

Being a side chick can be really hard at times, and it can get lonely—so you need to find something to do on the days when the dick isn't around. This is where Chapter 5 comes into play. You need to decide whether you're free to talk to and see other people, or if you want to take this time to work on yourself. Use this space to get your life together and focus on what you really want out of life.

That doesn't mean you can't have friends. In fact, your friends will come in handy during this time, so make sure to keep in contact with them. If you're like me and have more male friends than female friends, make sure those friendships are just that—friendships unless you're into something more.

(No judgment here— to each their own! Just a little FYI: Sharing dick is how STDs happen, so stay safe out here.)

Keep Your Mouth Shut & Play Smart

Even if you're a side chick and don't know the main chick, remember—this is a small world. Not everyone needs to know who you are or who you're messing with. To keep things discreet, you should come up with a code name for him that only you know.

This might seem like a lot, but as a side chick, you need to understand that these days, it's not just about what you know—it's about who you know. And just like actors and actresses can be blackballed, so can you. That's why you need to keep your mouth shut about whose man you're sleeping with.

Like my father used to tell me:

☞ "No one's business is everyone's business, and everyone's business is no one's business."

So please—shut the fuck up about what you're doing and who you're doing it with. Not everything is for everybody. It's not about being sneaky or hiding anything—it's about keeping some things to yourself.

In this lifestyle, you need to know how to play the game you chose to play. If you don't, you'll end up hurt in more ways than one—and trust me, it won't be funny.

Now, let me be clear—I'm not saying being a side chick is okay. But reality is reality. What you won't do, another chick will. And sometimes, you can do everything to keep your man happy, but at the end of the day, if he wants to go—he will go.

As long as you know in your heart that you did everything you could to make that man happy—that's all that matters.

Rule Number 11
Know Your Worth

Now that we've covered all the rules, what it takes to be a good side chick, and the different types of side chicks, it's time to talk to the main chick.

Main chicks, I know this book is about side chicks, but you need to understand why side chicks exist and how they came to be.

Side chicks exist because there are things the main chick isn't doing or isn't willing to do to keep her man happy. This pushes some men to turn to another woman to get what they need—whether it's to feel like a man again, to boost their ego, or simply to fill a void.

Now, let's be real—sometimes, a man just likes to cheat. And in some cases, that's exactly what it is.

Why I Wrote This Book

I know all of you are wondering, *Why did I write this book?*

Are you a side chick?

Is that why you wrote this?

Are you trying to teach other women how to be side chicks like you?

The answer is yes to the first part of the question.

I was a side chick, but I didn't know I was the side chick.

    1. He lived with me and came home to me every night.

2. He never acted like I was the side chick.

At the end of the day, though, I was the side chick.

This man had a whole family on the other side that I knew nothing about.

Now, I know you're probably asking yourself, *How the hell did you not know this man had a wife and kid?*

Here's how:

- He lived with me.

- We were always on the phone.

- If he missed my call, he called right back—every single time.

- No matter the time—2 AM or 5 PM—it was always, *"Hey, babe."*

So, I didn't know. And yet, five years into the relationship, I found out I was nothing more than the side chick.

The Reason Behind This Book

It's that easy to be a side chick. And anyone can become one—even when you think you're the main chick.

This book is based on my real-life experiences—the things I went through that shaped me into the woman I am today.

Some of you may agree with this book. Some of you may not—and that's fine.

But at the end of the day, my money is green, and it's accepted everywhere.

And just so you know—never judge a book by its cover.

Because who are you to judge me? Have you ever walked a mile in my shoes?

Until you do—go kick rocks with no shoes or socks and fuck up your feet.

Rule Number 12
Side Chick Application

This is just an example of what a side chick contract would look like. Some people use them, some people don't—it's all up to you.

Personal Information

Name:

Address:

City:

State:

Zip Code:

Phone Number:

Email Address:

Position Title:

Start Date:

Educational Background

Name of School(s):

- Name of School:

- Name of School:

- Name of School:

Degree Earned:

Work History

Work History (1):

Company Name and Address:

Company's Phone Number (including Manager's Office Number):

Company's Complete Address:

Position Held:

Work History (2):

Company Name and Address:

Company's Phone Number (including Manager's Office Number):

Company's Complete Address:

Position Held:

Work History (3):

Company Name and Address:

Company's Phone Number (including Manager's Office Number):

Company's Complete Address:

Position Held:

Work History (4):

Company Name and Address:

Company's Phone Number (including Manager's Office Number):

Company's Complete Address:

Position Held:

Additional Information

List of all friends (first and last names, including nicknames):

Areas in which your family lives (state and city):

Type of vehicle you drive (year, make, model, and tag number):

Rule Number 13
The NDA Form and Its Importance

Now, this rule should really explain itself, but let me break it down for you. By both parties signing this paperwork, it stops the other person from putting your business out there for the world to see. To break it down even more, here's an example:

If you like to send pictures to each other or if you both make a video, what is stopping him/her from posting or leaking it? Nothing.

And if you fall for that "But I love you and would never hurt you" BS, then you need to go back to rule number one, reread it, and think about that for a minute. I'm sure the first person you fell in love with said the same thing, right? Now ask yourself—are you still with that person, or are you with someone new?

If the answer is that you're with someone new, then you already know people lie—that's just facts. Both men and women lie, so don't fall for that shit. Protect yourself at all costs because, best believe, that man's girl, wife, baby mama—hell, even his mom—will try to destroy your life once they find out you're messing with their man.

Yes, some guys' moms act like they're in a relationship with their sons. Sick, I know, but shit happens. So, protect yourself at all costs.

Here is an attached copy of an NDA (Non-Disclosure Agreement) to give you an idea of what it should look like. You can make changes to it to match your needs or situation.

NON-DISCLOSURE AGREEMENT

PARTIES

- This Non-Disclosure Agreement (hereinafter referred to as the **"Agreement"**) is entered into on _____ (the **"Effective Date"**), by and between _____, with an address of _____, (hereinafter referred to as the **"Disclosing Party"**) and _____, with an address of _____, (hereinafter referred to as the **"Receiving Party"**) (collectively referred to as the **"Parties"**).

CONFIDENTIAL INFORMATION

- The Receiving Party agrees not to disclose, copy, clone, or modify any confidential information related to the Disclosing Party and agrees not to use any such information without obtaining consent.

- "Confidential information" refers to any data and/or information that is related to the Disclosing Party, in any form, including, but not limited to, oral or written. Such confidential information includes, but is not limited to, any information related to the business or industry of the Disclosing Party, such as discoveries, processes, techniques, programs, knowledge bases, customer lists, potential customers, business partners, affiliated partners, leads, know-how, or any other services related to the Disclosing Party.

RETURN OF CONFIDENTIAL INFORMATION

- The Receiving Party agrees to return all the confidential information to the Disclosing Party upon the termination of this Agreement.

OWNERSHIP

- This Agreement is not transferable and may only be transferred by written consent provided by both Parties.

GOVERNING LAW

- This Agreement shall be governed by and construed in accordance with the laws of _____.

SIGNATURE AND DATE

- The Parties hereby agree to the terms and conditions set forth in this Agreement and such is demonstrated by their signatures below:

Rule Number 14
When It's Time to Let Go

When you see things starting to change between you and the guy, it's time to do one of two things. Option one: Change the agreement between the two of you to make sure it still works for both parties. Option two: Walk away and let him go—because if you don't, things can start to get messy, and no one wants that.

I know that sometimes side chicks and their guys may have an arrangement that lasts for years, while other times, the deal only lasts a few weeks. It all depends on you and what works for your situation. What works for someone else may not work for you, and if something doesn't sit right with you, you need to make that clear.

And it's okay if this is just something you're doing while healing or working on yourself. No one sets out to be a side chick, but sometimes, being a side chick isn't necessarily a bad thing—it may actually be what you need to heal. Yeah, I know healing is about working on yourself and figuring out who you are as a person, but in a way, being a side chick can teach you just that.

You learn what you like and don't like. You see how guys lie and manipulate with words. You start to recognize the games they play. And at the same time, you're protecting yourself because you already know what it is—there's an understanding.

Now, I'm sure a lot of women won't agree with what I'm saying. Some will argue that we, as women, need to stand together and support each other—that sleeping with another woman's man is wrong and that we should care about her feelings.

But let me ask you something—how many women can honestly say they've never taken or slept with another woman's man? I don't care if it was back in elementary school or as an adult. As kids, we were taught to fight for what we want—so what makes this any different?

Hell, let's be real—relationships aren't what they used to be. Nowadays, it's more about "What can I get out of this?" than it is about love. And at the end of the day, you have no idea what he told that other woman to get things started in the first place.

www.ingramcontent.com/pod-product-compliance
Lightning Source LLC
Chambersburg PA
CBHW051307140626
46546CB00020B/1569